A Dog Called Bear

Story by Annette Smith
Illustrations by Richard Hoit

NELSON PRICE MILBURN

Bear put his nose
around the classroom door
and padded in.

"Matthew!" called Henry.
"Bear's here!"

Bear was a big, brown dog.
He belonged to Matthew,
who lived next door to the school.
Henry gave Bear a hug,
but Matthew looked cross.

"I'm going to have to take
you home, Bear," said Matthew.

"Henry, you can go with Matthew," said Mr Ford.
"Please be quick, boys."

The boys walked
across the school playing field.
Matthew had his hand
on Bear's collar.

"Bear, you **know** you can't come
to school," Matthew said crossly.
"Come on. Hurry up!"

Bear looked up at Matthew
and just wagged his tail.
He was an old dog
and he didn't like hurrying.

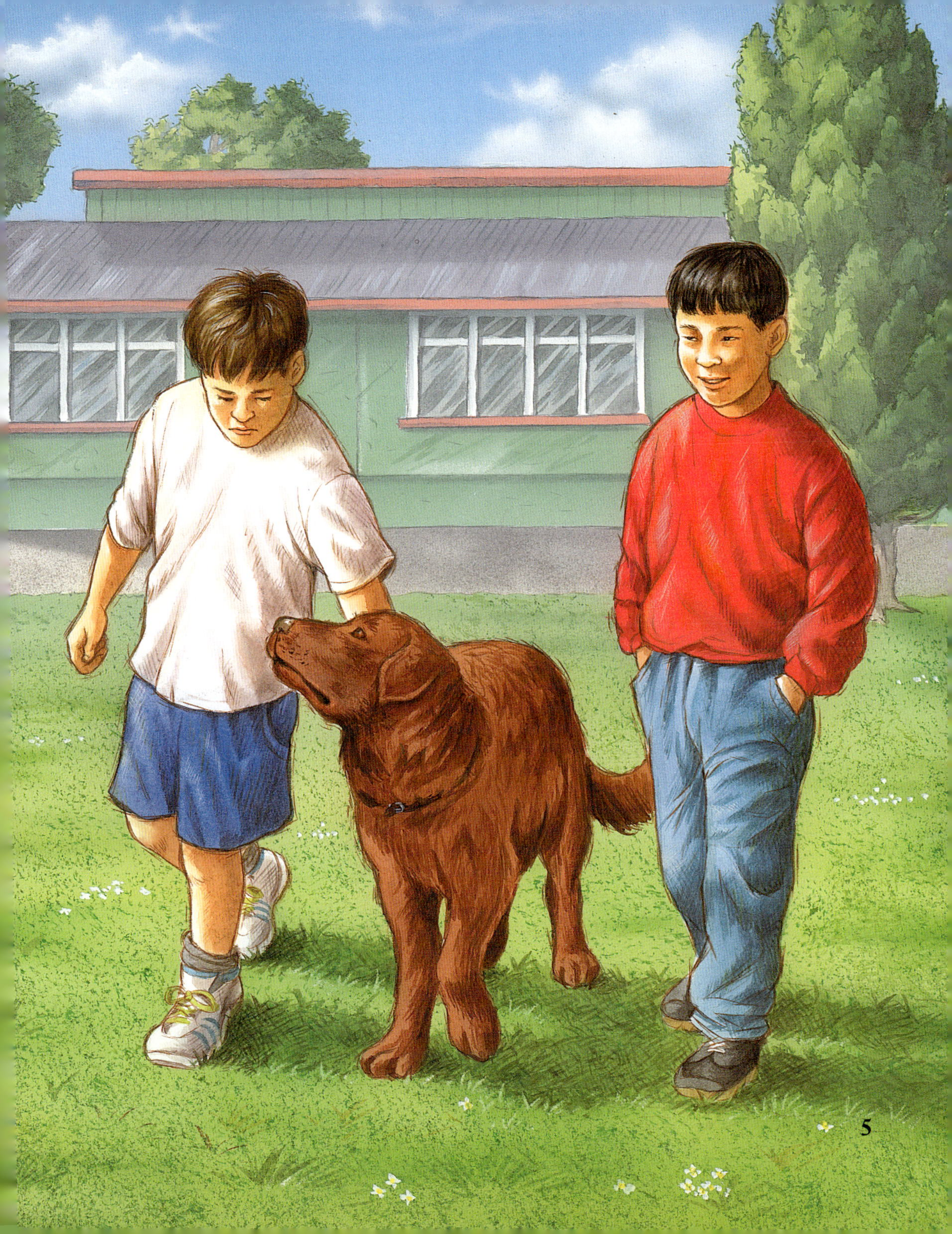

Bear was a friendly old dog.
The children at school loved him.
When they went over to the fence
to talk to him,
Bear always wagged his tail
and seemed to smile at them.

"Now stay here, Bear," said Matthew,
as he shut the gate behind him.
"I'll be home later."

Bear looked sad as he put his head
on his paws and watched the boys
running back to the classroom.

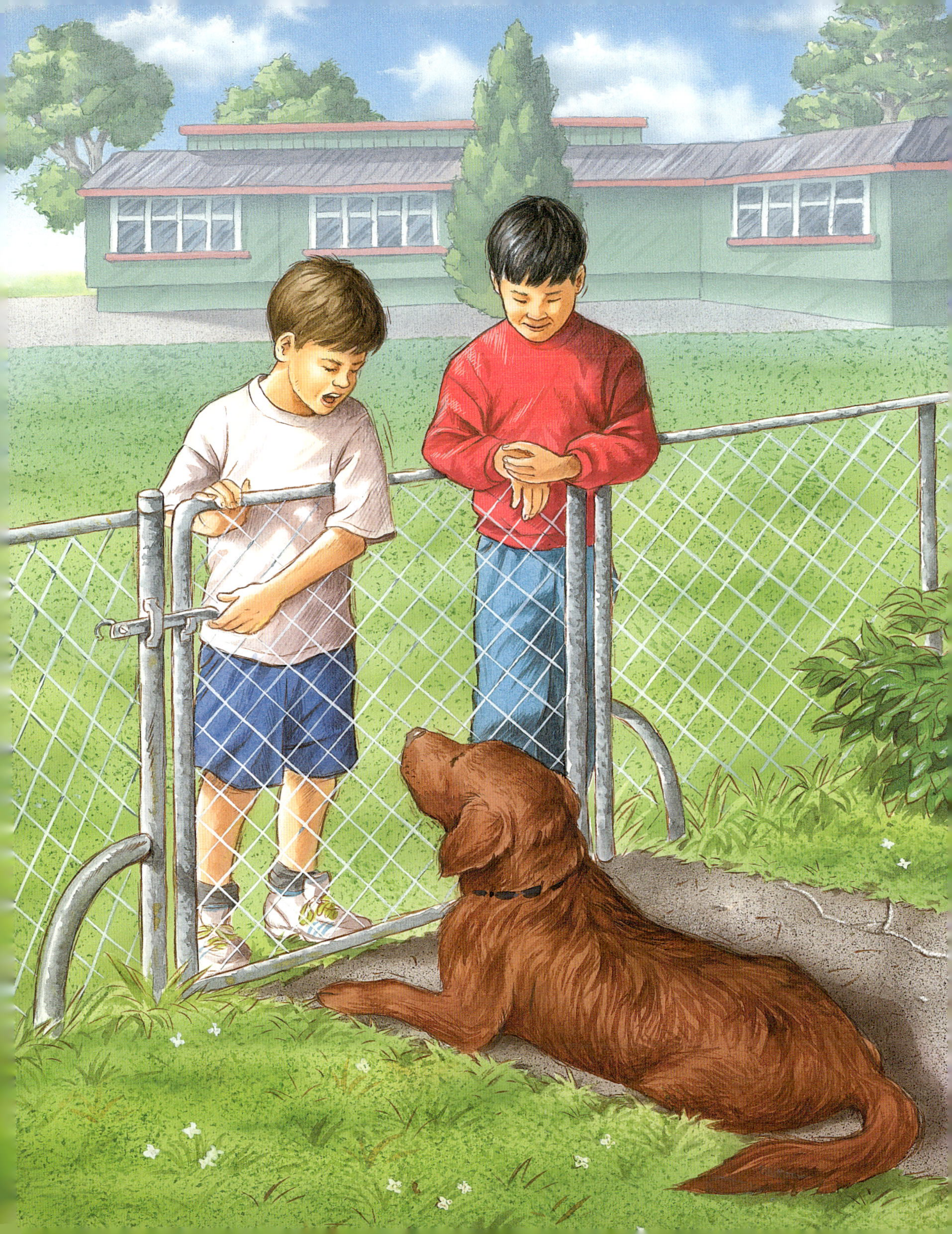

A little while later, Henry whispered, "Hey, Matthew! Bear's come back."

"Not again!" groaned Matthew.
"How **did** he get out?
Mr Ford, Bear's here **again**.
Henry saw him going past
the window.
Can I go and get him, please?"

Suddenly, they heard a squeal of brakes.
Everyone rushed to the window.

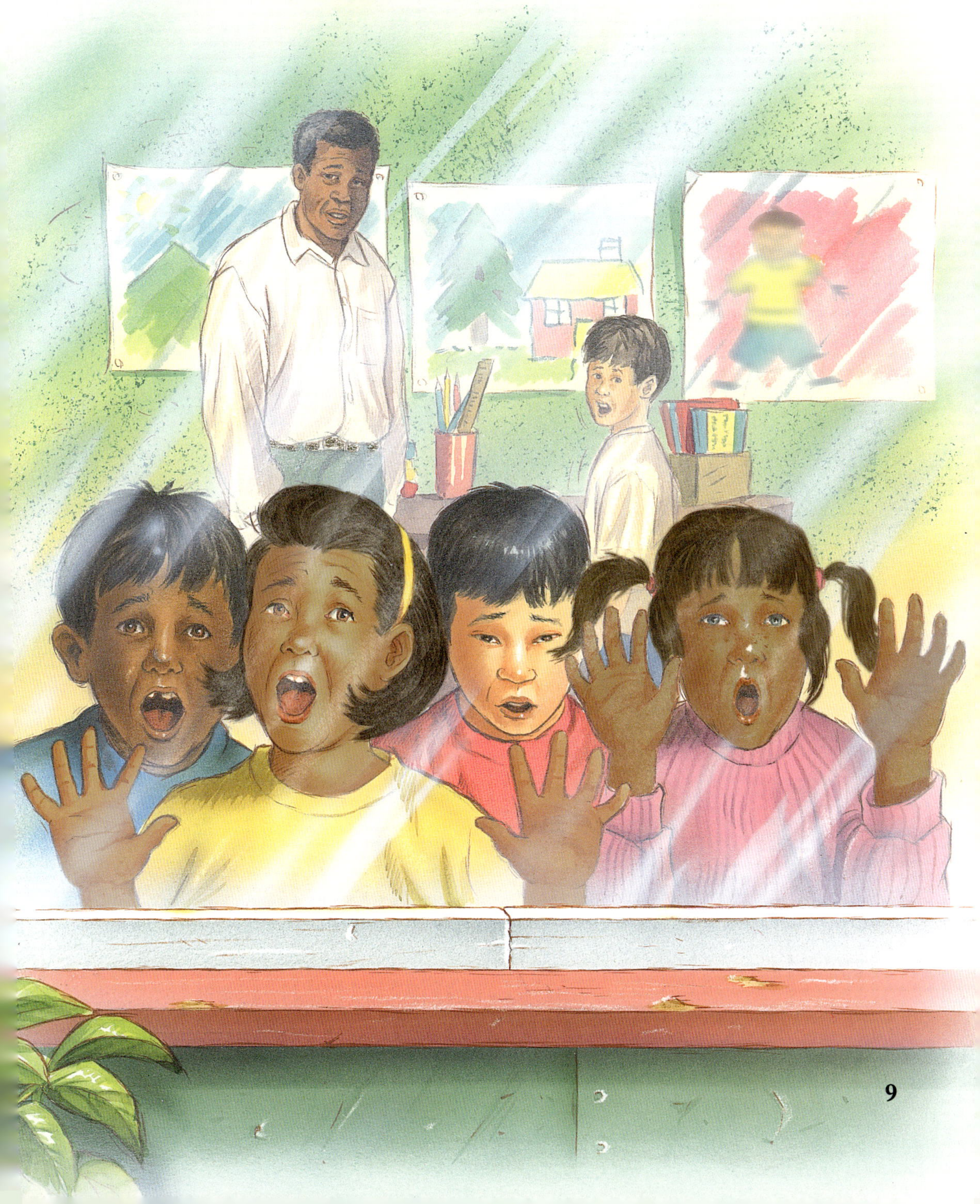

A car had stopped
at the school crossing
and Bear was lying on the road.

"Bear's been hit!" cried Henry.

"Stay here, children," said Mr Ford.

The principal came hurrying
out to the crossing
to see what had happened.
Some parents were standing nearby,
and one mother was holding
a little girl who was crying.

Bear lifted his head
and staggered to his feet.

An older girl from another class
came to get Matthew.

"Bear looks as if he's all right,"
said Mr Ford.
"Henry, you can go out
with Matthew, too."

"I hope Bear isn't badly hurt," said Matthew,
as they raced down the path towards the crossing.

By now, Bear was walking around.
His legs were shaky,
but he wagged his tail hard
when he saw Matthew.

"The car just gave him
a little bump,"
said the principal.

"Is this your dog?"
said the mother
to Matthew.
"He stopped my little girl
from running out
on to the road."

15

"How did he do it?" asked Matthew. "Bear can't run very fast!"

"He did this time," said the driver of the car.

"Bear's a hero!" said Henry.

"Bear's our best friend!" said Matthew. "I'm glad he came to school today."